The 'Parents' Time Off' Series

KIDS' MAGICAL ACTIVITIES

Cecilia Egan
Illustrated by Christine Eddy

First published in 1989 by Ashton Egan
as The Kids' First Book of Magical Activities

Revised and updated 2015
Copyright © Leaves of Gold Press 2015
The right of Cecilia Egan to be identified as author of this work has been
asserted in accordance with the Copyright, Designs and Patents Act, 1988.

National Library of Australia Cataloguing-in-Publication entry:

Creator: Egan, Cecilia, author.

Title: Kids' magical activities / Cecilia Egan ; Christine Eddy, illustrator.

Edition: 2nd edition

ISBN: 9781925110685 (paperback)

Series: Parents' time off series ; 1.

Target Audience: For primary school age (6-12 year old)

Subjects: Magic tricks--Juvenile literature.

Other Creators/Contributors: Eddy, Christine, illustrator.

Dewey Number: 793.8

LEAVES of GOLD PRESS ®

ABN 67 099 575 078

PO Box 9113, Brighton, 3186, Victoria, Australia
www.leavesofgoldpress.com

INTRODUCTION

Kids' Magical Activities is full of fun illusions to amaze and entertain your friends. The tricks are easy for six to twelve year olds to do, and those which take a little more practice are marked with a star.
   * Very easy
   ** Easy
   *** Needs some practice

You will not need any special equipment, only objects which are usually found around the home. These things are written in **bold type** so that you know at a glance what you will need.

Have fun!

CONTENTS

X-RAY EYES*

Make believe you have X-ray vision!

Cut two small **cardboard** circles with **scissors**.

1. Fix a **hair** to one with **sticky tape**, then use **glue** to stick the cardboard circles together.

2. Cut three cardboard shapes as shown. Fold into pointed hats, tape joins together and decorate with **paint**.

Doing the Trick

Ask someone to cover the circle with one hat while you look the other way. When you turn around, look for the hair sticking out from under one of the hats.

Then you can say which hat hides the circle.

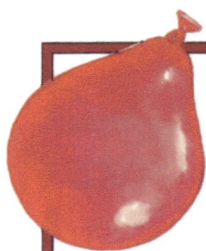

PINCUSHION BALLOON*

This specially-prepared **balloon** won't burst when you push in a **pin** at the right place!

Put a square of transparent **sticky tape** on a balloon that you have blown up.

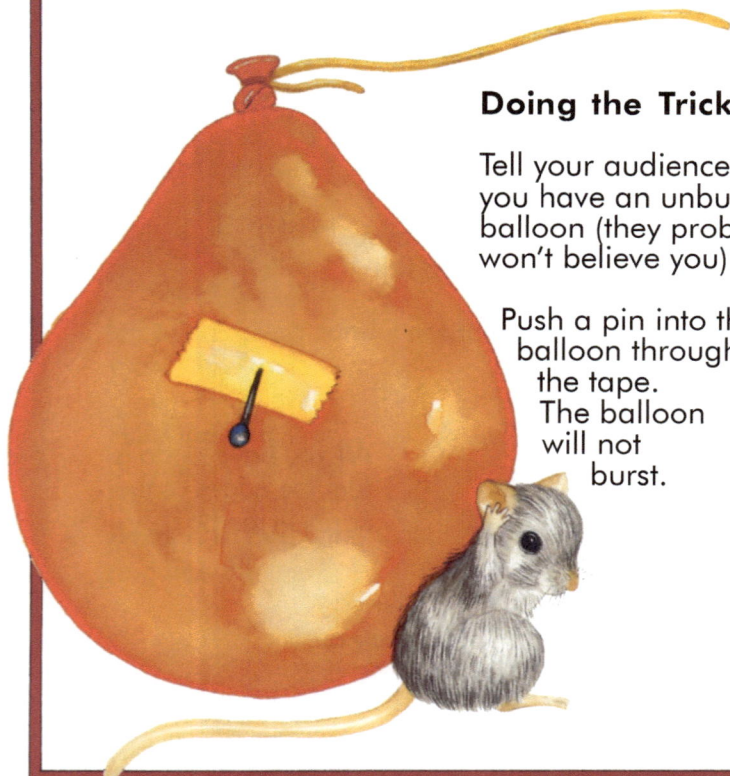

Doing the Trick

Tell your audience that you have an unburstable balloon (they probably won't believe you).

Push a pin into the balloon through the tape. The balloon will not burst.

ICE-CREAM AND JELLY*

No secret preparation is needed for this trick.

Use a **pencil** to write the words 'ice-cream', 'jelly', 'ice-cream' on a thin piece of **cardboard**.
Tear the card in three and put the pieces into a **box**

Tell your friends you can read the words without looking, then close your eyes and pick the card which says 'jelly'.

Picking the right card is easy. Because it is in the middle, the 'jelly' card has two jagged edges when torn.

All you have to do is feel the edges of the cards in the box!

3

DISAPPEARING RING**

Keep this trick up your sleeve for when you and your friends are feeling bored.

Tie a **piece of elastic** to a **ring**. The elastic should be about three-quarters the length of your arm.

1. Tie the other end of the elastic to a **safety-pin**. Fasten the pin inside the top of the right **sleeve of .your jumper** (sweater).

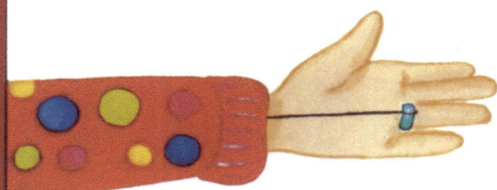

2. Put the ring on one of your right fingers and then put your jumper on.

3. Take the ring off your finger with the left hand, being careful not to show the elastic.

Hold the ring between your right forefinger and thumb.
Pretend to throw the ring into the air.

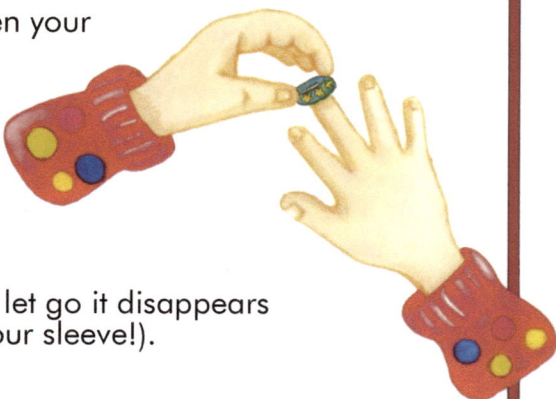

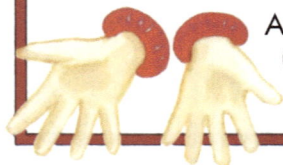

As you let go it disappears (up your sleeve!).

GENIUS*

You don't have to practise this trick -
iust look confident and your friends
will think you are a genius!

Using **scissors**, cut some **paper** into slips, and ask
your audience to call out different names. With a **pen**,
write iust one of the names on all the slips of paper.

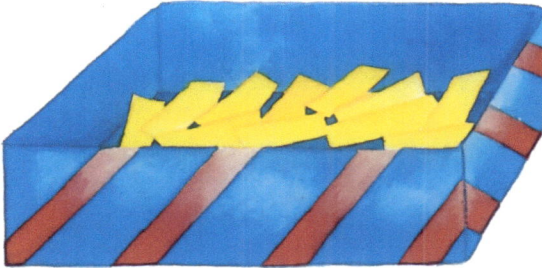

Your audience will think you are writing down each of
the different names as they are called out. Put all the
slips into a b**ox with a lid**, and shake the box.

Ask someone to take out one
slip of paper, but tell them not
to show it to you. Throw away
all the slips of paper. Now you
can tell everyone the name on
the slip!

MAGNETIC HAND **

This **pencil** seems to stick to your hand.

Show the audience a **pencil** in your left hand, turn-
ing the back of your hand towards them.

Grasp your left wrist with your right hand. The spec-
tators now see the pencil stuck to it.

What nobody sees is your right forefinger holding
the pencil in your left palm.

Move your finger to roll the pencil slightly back and
forth, and it seems to hover.

BOUNCING COIN*

Make a **coin** move without touching itl

Place a small coin on top of a **bottle that has some lemonade or other gassy drink in** it.

Hold the bottle tightly in both hands around the part that contains the drink.

The coin will begin to jump up and down.

The warmth of your hands makes the gas expand.

As it escapes from the bottle, it pushes up the coin.

PASS THE COIN*

You need a few people in your audience to be able to do this magical trick.

Put several **coins** in a **box.**

Tell your audience you can pick out a coin someone else chooses without seeing it first.

Ask someone to take out any coin while your back is turned.

Ask for the coin to be passed round so that everyone can look at it and remember it. Then the coin must be put back in the box.

When you turn around, feel about in the box for the warmest coin and take it out.

Everyone will be astonished when they see it is the right one.

OBEDIENT ICE-CUBE*

Learn to lift an ice-cube without touching it!

Ask someone to try and lift an ice-cube out of a glass of water with a piece of string, without touching the ice. He won't be able to do it, but you will.

Doing the Trick

Put an **ice-cube** in a **glass of water**.

1. Lay one end of **a piece of string** on top of the ice-cube.

2. Pour some **salt** on the icecube and the string. Wait a few seconds and then lift the string up.

3. The ice-cube will now stick to the string and can be lifted from the glass.

INVISIBLE WRITING*

Make someone's name appear as if by magic!

1. Soak a **sheet of paper** in **a tray of water,** then put the wet paper on a mirror or window.

2. Put **a dry sheet of paper** over the wet one.

3. With a **pencil**, write the name of a friend on the top sheet of paper.

4. Discard the top sheet and leave the bottom sheet to dry. The name will then be invisible.

Doing the Trick

5. Show the sheet of paper and say that you can make your friend's name appear on it.

6. Put the paper in the tray of water and the writing will show up!

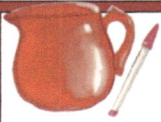

TWO-WAY STREET*

This very easy trick almost works by itself!

Use a **felt-tipped pen** to draw an arrow on a small piece of **cardboard.**

Put the cardboard behind a **glass tumbler.**

Ask a friend to !ook through the tumbler as you pour water into it.

When the tumbler is almost full the arrow will seem to turn and point in the other direction.

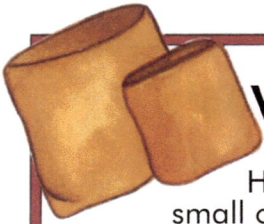

VANISHING WATCH*

Here's a way to make **a watch** (or any small object) disappear!

Use **glue** to stick the top of a **small paper bag** to the inside top of a **large paper bag**.

Doing the Trick

Show your audience the watch and tell them you can make it disappear.

1. Put the watch in the small paper bag (everyone will think it is in the big bag).

2. Blow up the big bag and burst it.

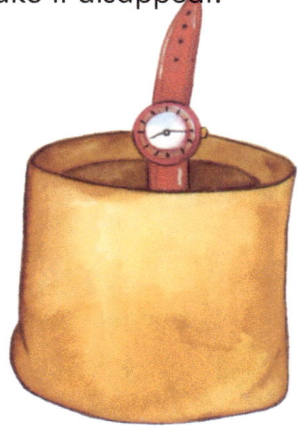

3. Show the empty torn bag. (The watch is still hidden in the small paper bag, but it will seem to have vanished.)

ASTONISHING RINGS*

For this trick you need to wear a jacket with pockets and wide sleeves.

Find two plastic bangles, exactly the same and big enough to fit over your arm.

Place one of the bangles over your hand and push it a little way up your sleeve, out of sight.

Doing the Trick

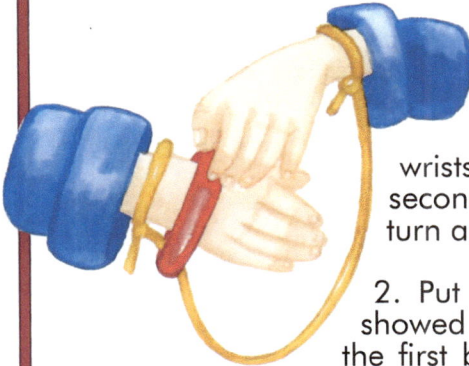

1. Give someone a length of rope and ask him or her to tie the ends to each of your wrists. Show the audience the second plastic bangle. Then turn around for a moment.

2. Put the plastic bangle you showed into your pocket. Pull the first bangle down from your sleeve and onto the rope.

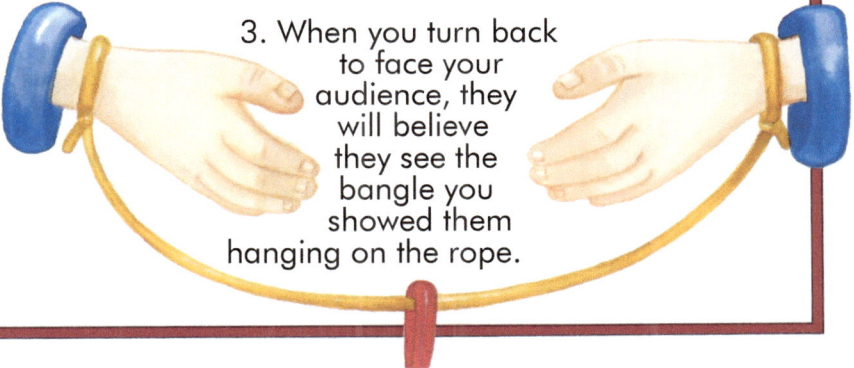

3. When you turn back to face your audience, they will believe they see the bangle you showed them hanging on the rope.

13

MAGICAL STRAW*

Turn a drinking straw into a magic wand.

1. Dip one end of the straw into some sugar. Use a cloth to wipe off the outside of the straw.

2. Dip the other end of the straw in soft soap. Wipe the straw again so the soap can't be seen.

Doing the Trick

Now show your friends how you can make two matchsticks move without touching them.

3. Place two dead matchsticks in a bowl of water.

4. Dip the sugared end of the straw into the water between the matches.
The matches will move close together.

5. Dip in the soapy end of the straw. The matches will move apart.

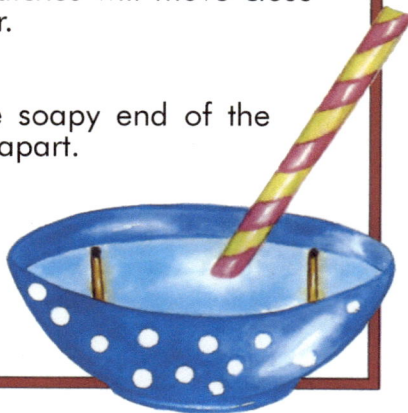

DOUBLE YOUR MONEY*

Tell your friends you can double their money!

1. Hide four coins inside the pages of a newspaper.
Hold the newspaper so they cannot fall out.

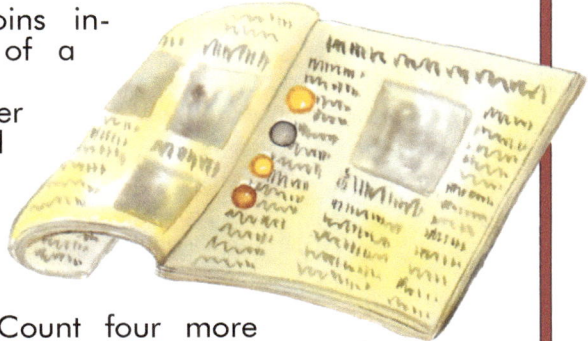

2. Count four more coins onto the newspaper and ask someone to hold out a hand.

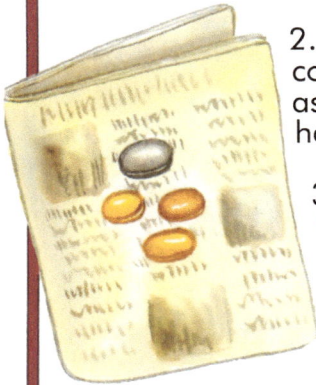

3. Tip the coins into the hand, making sure that the four extra coins from inside the newspaper fall out as well. Ask your friend to close his hand quickly.

When he opens his hand he will see he has eight coins!

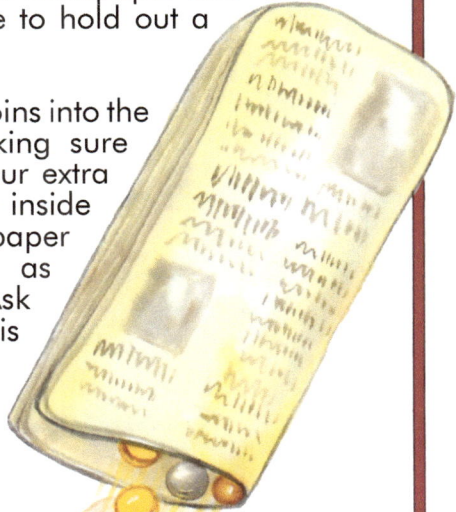

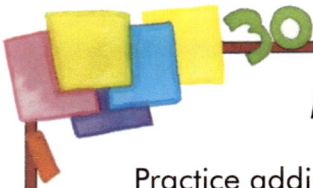

MATHEMAGIC**

Practice adding in your head, then copy these numbers in **pencil** on **five pieces of cardboard**.

Blue card:
9
5 7
1 3 17
19
13 15 29
11 25 27
21 23

Red card:
10
6 7
2 3 18
14 19
15 30
11 26
22 27
23

Yellow card:
12
6 7
4 20
5 21
14 30
13 15
22 28 29
23

Doing the Trick

Give all the cards to someone and say you can tell them any number he or she secretly chooses simply by looking at the cards.

1. Ask the person to think of any number between one and thirty and to give you back all the cards that carry the chosen number.

2. In your head, add up the numbers in the top lefthand corner of each of the cards that have been given back to you.

Your total will be the chosen number!

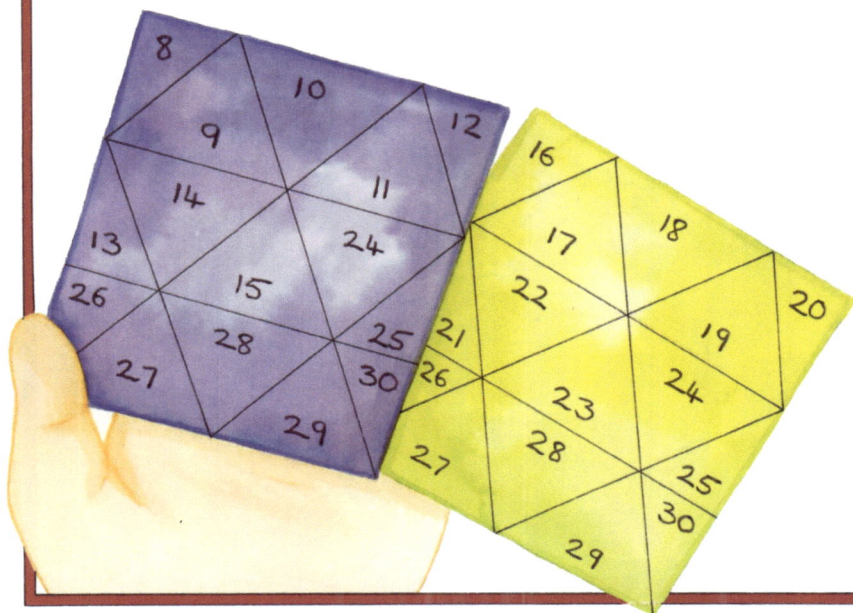

MELTING TABLE**

Practice this trick carefully before showing it!

Sit at a **table** facing your audience. Put a **glass tumbler** upside down on the table.

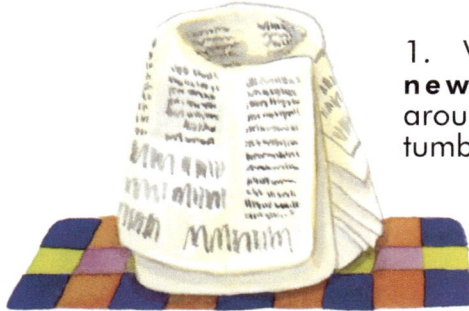

1. Wrap a **newspaper** around the tumbler.

2. With the right hand, move these to the edge of the table near you.

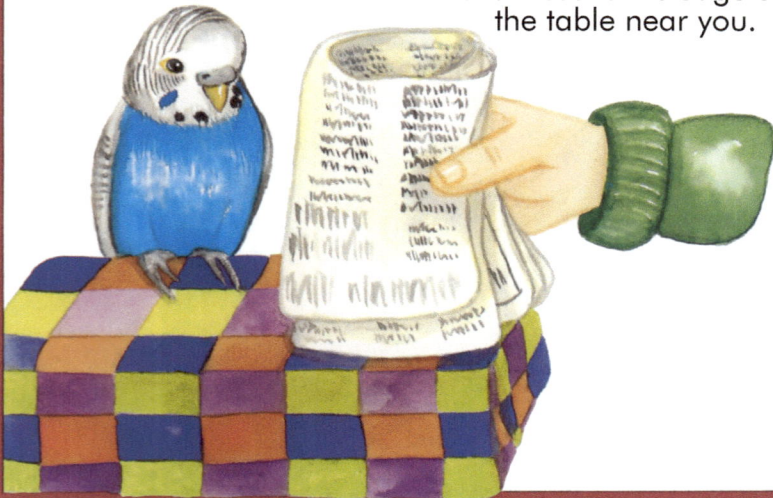

3. With the left hand point at the table top. At the same time let the tumbler drop from the paper on to your lap.

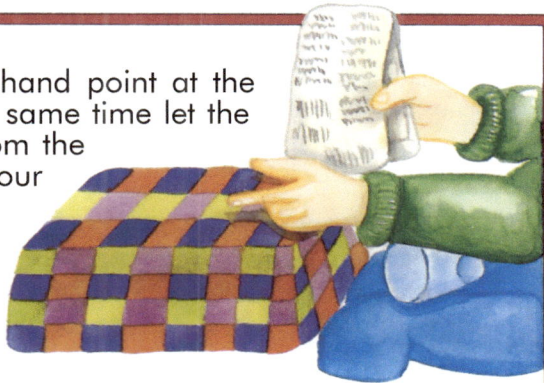

4. Move the empty paper to the centre of the table.
No one is aware that the tumbler is not in the paper.

Crush the paper onto the table top. Put your other hand under the table, so that it seems to be underneath the place where the paper is.

As you bring your hand back, pick up the tumbler from your lap and show it to the audience.

It looks as if the tumbler went straight through the table top!

BAGS OF LOLLIPOPS*

This trick works best if you practice it first.

With **scissors**, cut four discs out of **cardboard**. Use **poster paints or felt-tip pens** to colour one disc red, one blue, one green, and one yellow.

Put a **drinking straw** between the red and green discs, and stick them together with **glue**.

Glue the blue and yellow discs together over the other end of the straw. Put in a **paper bag**.

Doing the Trick

Take the 'lollipop' from the bag to show the red side. Hide the other end in your hand.

Put the lollipop back in the bag, twisting it around as you do so.

Take it out and show your audience a green lollipop, then put it back.

Take it out two more times to show first the
blue and then the yellow lollipops.

Always make sure the other end is hidden in your hand.

Take out the lollipop with the red side showing and drop it in a box.

Show the audience the empty paper bag.

The other lollipops have vanished!

MIND READING RIBBONS*

This trick should convince your friends that you have some very magical ribbons.

1. Use **small rubber bands** to join **three differently coloured ribbons** into a circle.

2. Put the ribbon circle into a **paper bag**.

You will need **three more ribbons the same colours** as the ones tied together.

Doing the Trick

Give the three spare ribbons to someone in your audience.

3. Ask the person to tie them into a long strip, but not to let you see it. Show everyone the paper bag.

Tell them it holds three ribbons which are able to tie themselves into the same order as the spare strips of ribbon.

4. Ask the person with the spare ribbons to hold up the strip.

Look at the colours showing at the top and bottom of the strip. (You must remember what the colours are.)

Put your hands into the bag and slip off the rubber band that ioins the two colours you noticed in the strip.

5. Take hold of the same colour as the other person is holding, and pull the ribbons from the bag.

The order of colours will be the samel

TRICKY TUBE *

Make things vanish and re-appear mysteriously!

With **scissors**, cut out three pieces of **thin cardboard**,

- 30cm by 30cm, (12" x 12")
- 30cm x 25cm (12" x 10") and
- 30cm by 20cm (12" x 8")

Bend the cardboard to make three tubes.

1. Fix the tube joins with **sticky tape**.
Decorate the outside of the two larger tubes with **poster paints or felt-tip pens**. Fit the three tubes inside one another.

2. Put a **coloured scarf** and some **ribbons** inside the smallest tube. Make sure that they cannot be seen by your audience.

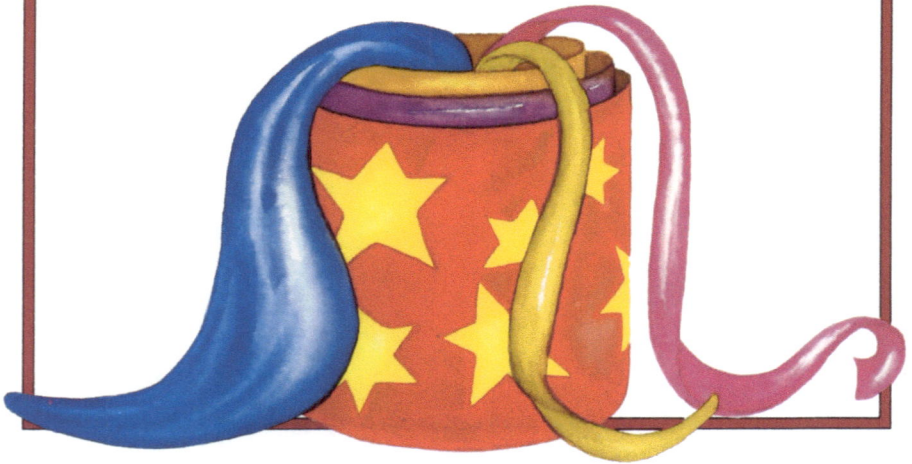

Doing the Trick

3. Take out the second tube and show the audience that it is empty. Put it back inside the large tube.

Now pick up the large tube and show it to be empty too.

4. Put the large tube back over the second tube. In this way the smallest tube is never seen by the audience.

5. Now amaze your audience by pulling out the ribbons and then the scarf.

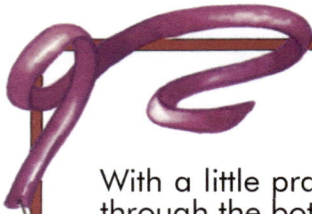

MYSTERIOUS GLASS*

With a little practice, you can seem to pull a ribbon through the bottom of a glass.

With a **needle**, sew 20cm (8") of **cotton thread** firmly to one end of a ribbon.

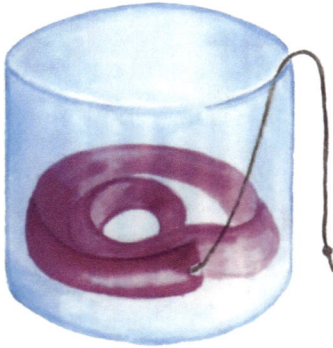

Tie several knots to make one large knot in the free end of the thread.

1. Show your audience a **glass tumbler** and drop the ribbon in it.

Make sure that the thread (which is invisible from a distance) is hanging over the edge of the glass.

2. Put a **handkerchief** over the glass. It must be big enough to cover the glass completely.

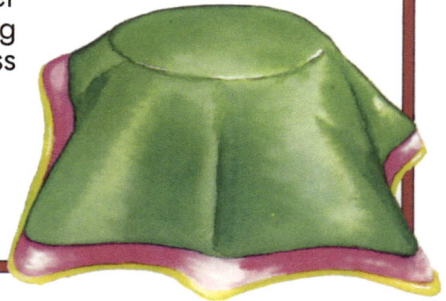

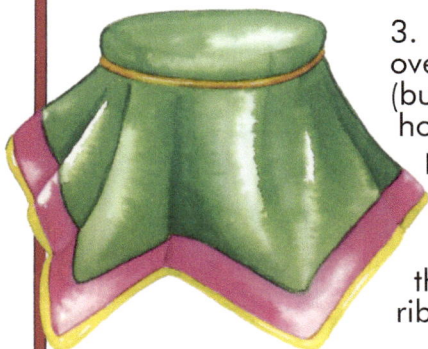

3. Put an **elastic band** over the rim of the glass (but not too tightly) to hold the handkerchief in position.

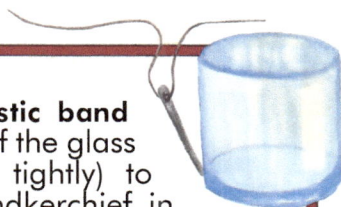

Put one hand under the handkerchief and pull the thread down. This draws the ribbon out of the glass.

4. Pull the ribbon out from beneath the handkerchief.

It looks as if it has been pulled through the bottom of the glass!

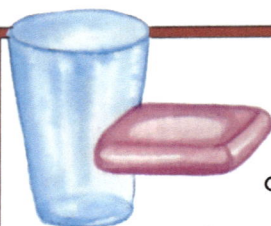

RISING CARD*

Command a playing card to rise out of a glass by itself!

1. Get **a fairly tall drinking glass**, slightly wider than a playing card at the top, but a lot narrower at the bottom.

2. Rub the inner walls of the glass with **soap** and spread it with your fingertips until you can hardly see it.

3. Choose a **playing card** from **a fairly new pack**. It must have a glossy or plastic finish so that the edges are smooth.

4. Push the card down into the glass and cover the glass with the pack.

5. Then lift the pack and say "Rise, card!" The card will rise up from the slippery glass by itself, and may even pop right out!

FLAP JACKPOT*

Here's a way to double your money!

1. Using **tracing paper** and a **pencil**, trace the shape shown here on to **two pieces of paper**. Use scissors to cut out the two shapes.

2. Fold along the dotted lines and stick the two papers back to back with **glue**.

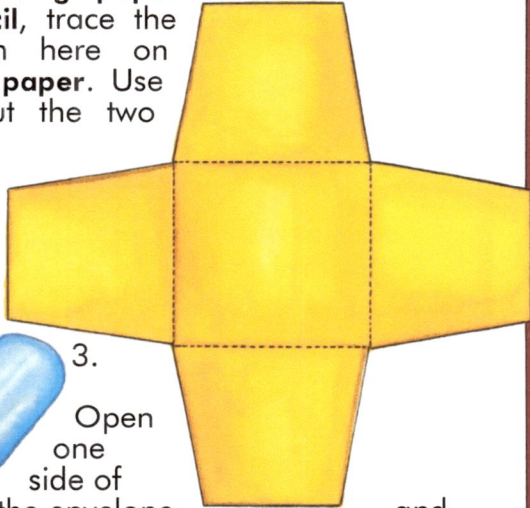

3. Open one side of the envelope and insert **two small coins**, then close the flaps.

Doing the Trick

Open the empty side of the envelope and show it to your audience. Show **a third coin**, of the same type as the two in the 'envelope'. Put this third coin in the envelope, and then close the flaps.

Say some magic words and turn around once as you secretly turn over your envelope. Open the flaps and show your audience two coins!

Leaves of Gold Press takes pride in publishing fantasy novels, children's books, and well-loved classic fiction for adults and young adults. We also offer top quality non-fiction, covering subjects from health and beauty to rare and unusual edible plants.

We are excited about what we do, we care about our customers and we strive always for improvement.

Our books are printed on high grade, acid-free, book-grade, opaque paper stock sourced from responsibly managed forests.

Our printers are certified by the Forest Stewardship Council™, the Sustainable Forestry Initiative® and the Programme for the Endorsement of Forest Certification™.

Utilizing POD technology reduces paper waste, thereby cutting down greenhouse emissions and conserving valuable natural resources.

LEAVES of GOLD PRESS ®

The best books for adults, young adults and children.

www.leavesofgoldpress.com

The 'Parents' Time Off' Series

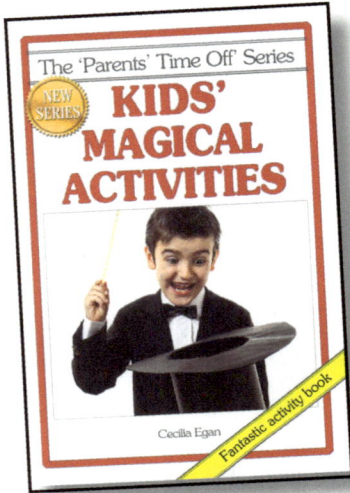

The 'Parents' Time Off' Series

NEW SERIES

KIDS' MAGICAL ACTIVITIES

Cecilia Egan

Fantastic activity book

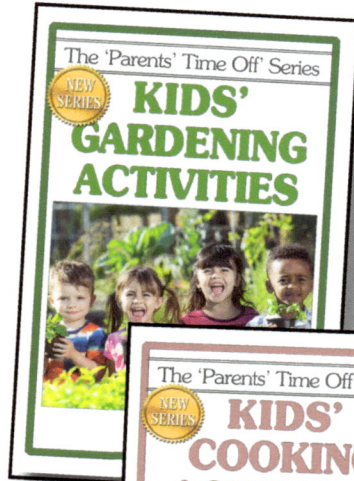

The 'Parents' Time Off' Series

NEW SERIES

KIDS' GARDENING ACTIVITIES

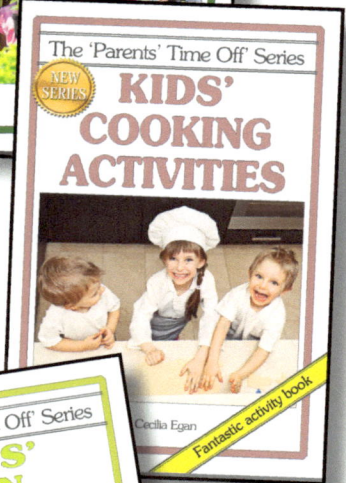

The 'Parents' Time Off' Series

NEW SERIES

KIDS' COOKING ACTIVITIES

Cecilia Egan

Fantastic activity book

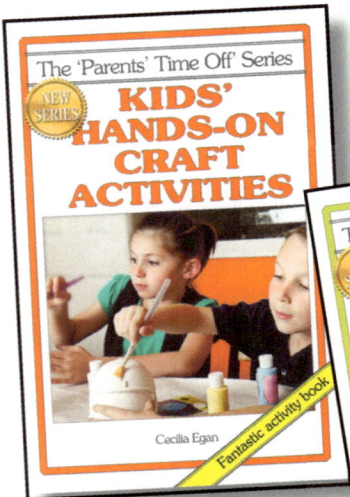

The 'Parents' Time Off' Series

NEW SERIES

KIDS' HANDS-ON CRAFT ACTIVITIES

Cecilia Egan

Fantastic activity book

The 'Parents' Time Off' Series

NEW SERIES

KIDS' FUN CRAFT ACTIVITIES

Cecilia Egan

Fantastic activity book

Fantastic activity books — no more school holiday boredom!

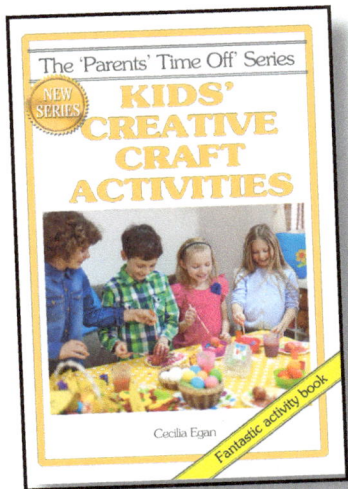

The 'Parents' Time Off' Series

KIDS' CREATIVE CRAFT ACTIVITIES

Cecilia Egan

Fantastic activity book

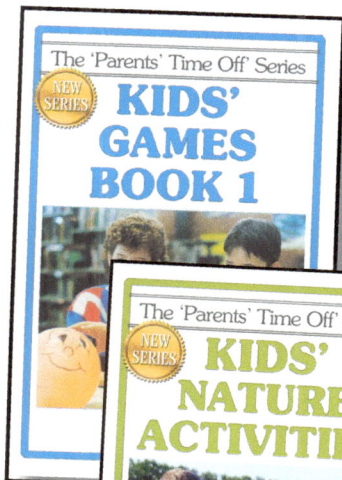

The 'Parents' Time Off' Series

KIDS' GAMES BOOK 1

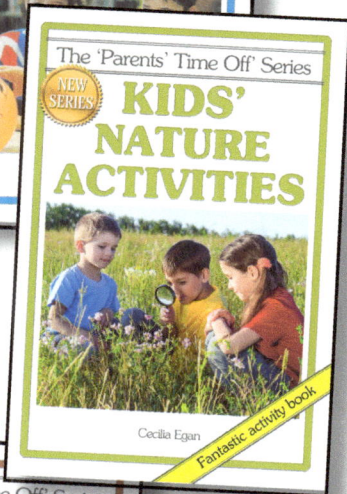

The 'Parents' Time Off' Series

KIDS' NATURE ACTIVITIES

Cecilia Egan

Fantastic activity book

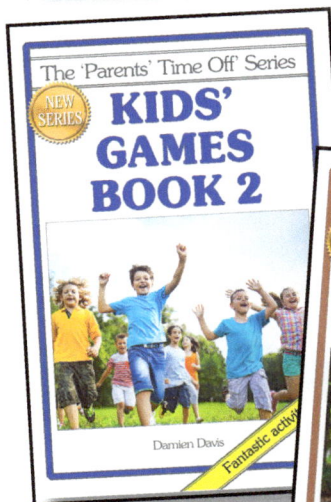

The 'Parents' Time Off' Series

KIDS' GAMES BOOK 2

Damien Davis

Fantastic activity book

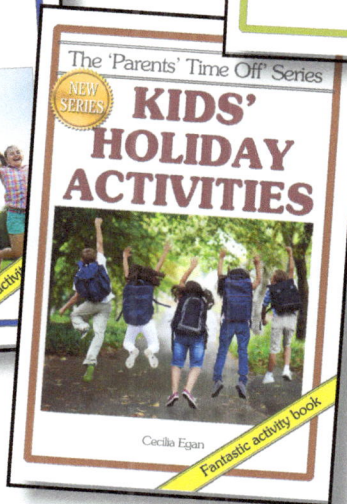

The 'Parents' Time Off' Series

KIDS' HOLIDAY ACTIVITIES

Cecilia Egan

Fantastic activity book

Princess Pam
Fell Into the Jam

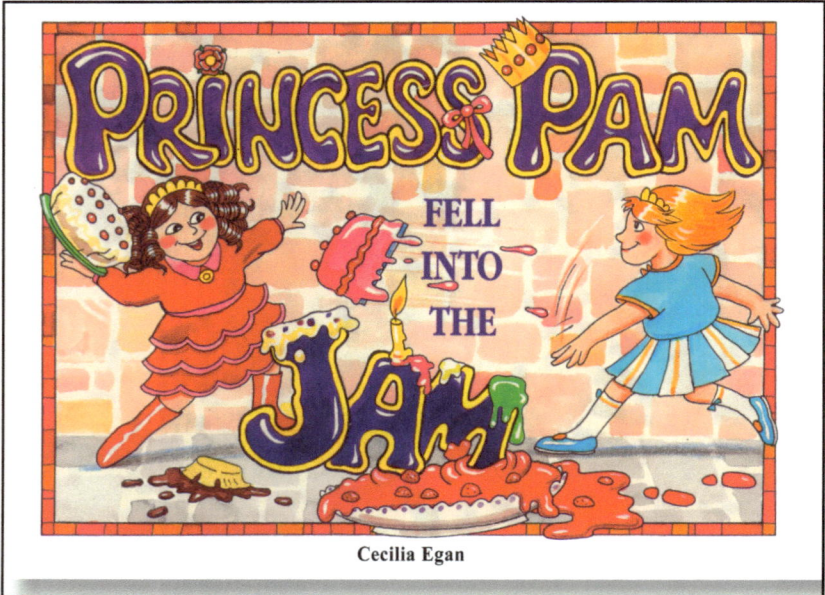

Cecilia Egan

More than a hilarious rhyme, this is a slapstick comedy that causes a riot of laughter when read aloud. Princess Pam and her messy sisters appeal to every child.

The rollicking rhymes, the unconventional story and the lively, detailed pictures combine to make one of the funniest and most original children's books published.

Princess Pam
and the Twenty-eight Brave Princes

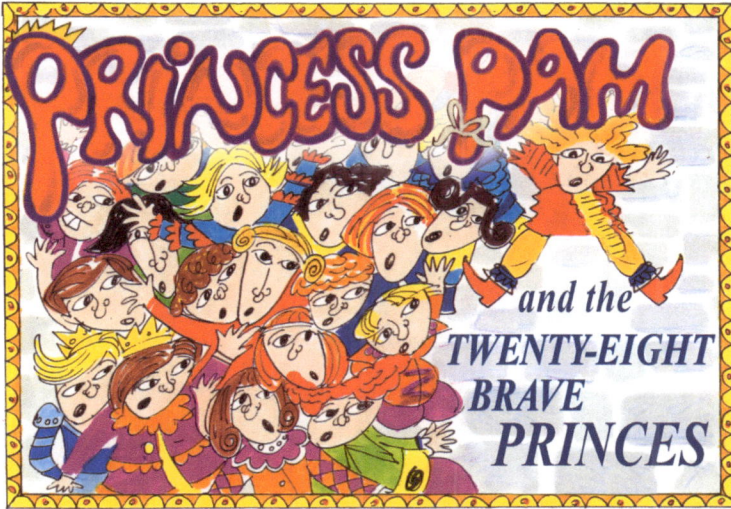

In this, the second in the riotous "Princess Pam" series, Princess Pam becomes involved in more uproarious, slapstick comedy when she and her naughty sisters and cousins meet the Brave Princes.

Classic Fairytales from Tolkien's Bookshelf

- Grimms' Fairytales - Illustrated
- The Red Fairy Book - Illustrated
- The Princess and the Goblin - Illustrated.
- The Story of King Arthur and his Knights - Illustrated

Find out more on our website!

www.leavesofgoldpress.com

The Fairytale Sequels

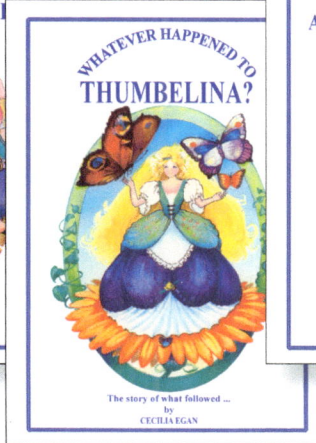

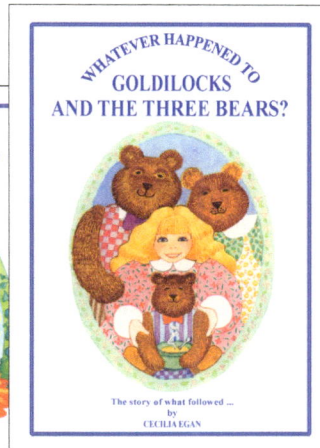

WHATEVER HAPPENED TO
THE THREE LITTLE P[I...]

The story of what followed ...
by
CECILIA EGAN

WHATEVER HAPPENED TO
THUMBELINA?

The story of what followed ...
by
CECILIA EGAN

WHATEVER HAPPENED TO
GOLDILOCKS
AND THE THREE BEARS?

The story of what followed ...
by
CECILIA EGAN

The Nursery Rhyme Stories

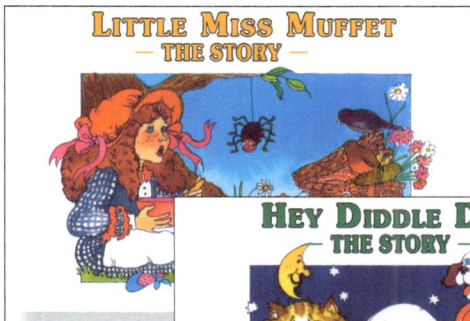

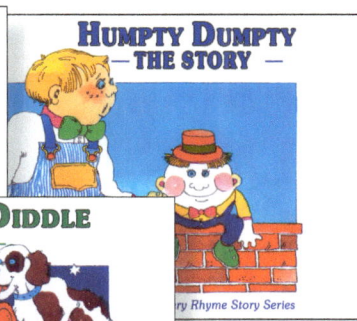

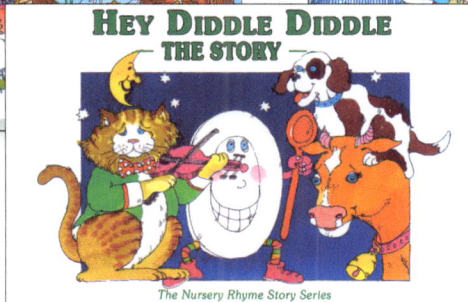

LITTLE MISS MUFFET
— THE STORY —

HUMPTY DUMPTY
— THE STORY —

...ry Rhyme Story Series

HEY DIDDLE DIDDLE
THE STORY

The Nursery Rhyme Story Series

www.ingramcontent.com/pod-product-compliance
Lightning Source LLC
Chambersburg PA
CBHW041215270326
41930CB00001B/32